UPROOTED

*A Poetic Journey Through
Seasons of Life*

Nicole N. (Nicci) Roach

UPROOTED

*A Poetic Journey Through
Seasons of Life*

Nicole N. (Nicci) Roach
nicciroach.com

UPROOTED
A Poetic Journey Through Seasons of Life

Copyright © 2024 by Nicole N. (Nicci) Roach

All rights reserved. No part of this publication may be reproduced, distributed, or transmitted in any form or by any means, including photocopying, recording, or other electronic or mechanical methods, without the prior written permission of the publisher, except in the case of brief quotations embodied in critical reviews and certain other non-commercial uses permitted by copyright law.

Disclaimer

The views and opinions expressed in this collection of poetry are those of the author and do not necessarily reflect the official policy or position of any organization, publisher, or institution. The contents are intended for inspirational and artistic purposes and should not be considered professional advice in any capacity.

For, Rev. Dr. Charles M. Roach and Lady Delores A. Roach, always.

Thank you for demonstrating how and equipping me to bloom in *every* season - winter's stillness, springs renewal, summer's warmth, and fall's transformation.

Uproot

/ˌəpˈroōt/

verb

1. to remove as if by pulling up
2. to pull up by the roots
3. move (someone) from their home or a familiar location.
4. to remove a person from their home or usual environment.
5. to displace from a country or traditional habitat

Contents

Author's Note 1
Stripped 5
Which Way 6
What Was It? 7
Outward In 9
The Audition 11
Realizing 12
In the Garden 13
It Hurts 14
Fight on 17
Under Construction 18
Shuffle the Cards 19
Like a Tree 21
Mirrored Image 21
Now Hiring 24
Grin and Bear 26
Between You and Me 27
Halt 31
Beef Stew 32
Not Known 33

Out of Sight	34
Big Girl	35
Tug of War	38
That's Friendship	42
Strength in Weakness	44
A Met Need	46
As if the Seasons	47
Simple Things	48
Dance I Said	50
Free-Dome	52
Go Get It	53
Go on	55
Great Expectation	56
She in Me	58
Hidden Treasure	59
I Imagined	62
Help	64
Shoe Shine	66
Delight Disorder	68
Mother's Touch	70
My Brother, My Lover, My King	73

Author's Note

There are thousands of known kinds of flowers. All start as either a seed or a bulb. They do no good if they aren't planted into a foundation. A bulb can eventually rot if not planted. The condition of the foundation is crucial; however, it doesn't always predict the outcome.

Once the seed or bulb is planted, needs must be met to begin the
growth process. Some require large amounts of water, some need fertilizer, some a cool

climate, some a hot climate, some shade, and some direct sun and others well-drained soil. With this in mind, not all can be mixed when planted since each requires individual, distinct provisions.

Not all will be planted or flourish in the same season. Take, for instance, the tulip. It's a flower that grows in spring but is planted in the fall. Perennials are planted in spring and fall and bloom the following year. Biennials are planted in midsummer and the flowers bloom the next spring.

After the seeds and/or bulbs are sown, the process of growth must occur. If you revisit this foundation periodically, you will notice the stem sprouting up higher and a circular shape right at the tip. With the right nurturing, this enclosed circular portion at the tip of the stem one day finally exposes that which had been hidden. The circular shape opens which is known as blooming.

Blooming is defined as flourishing, growing, developing, glowing, and radiant, which is the next phase of the flower. Looking over the foundation in which the seeds or bulbs were planted, no two flowers will be exactly the same. There will be something that will cause each one to be unique, standing out from the rest. The flowers are beautiful and appealing. Not only until the flowers are

UPROOTED, the purpose is fulfilled, a fresh bouquet.

To pull up by the roots, to remove entirely, displace, evacuate, to move on, to relocate is how the dictionary defines the word uprooted. It is a verb so that means action is behind this word. One flower alone can be eye-catching but it doesn't compare to many put together. When a fresh bouquet is delivered and given to someone, much cheer, appreciation, and delight is dispelled. When tears form and a smile spreads across the face of the recipient, the purpose has been accomplished.

The flower goes through a growth process before it reaches the point of purpose. We, just like the flower, must do the same. We start as seeds, later developing into unique characters. There may be another with similar interests, physical attributes, and more but no exact duplicate. No matter what shape or color of a flower, it represents beauty just like you and me. For each, there is a season to fulfill the purpose we are to carry out. The purpose is manifested in the flower, and you and I once we've been UPROOTED.

Stripped

So much pride she had and all.
Head up high. No plans to fall.

Had a vision as well as a dream.
Oh, so close they all seemed.

She began to walk the path of life.
This began the heartaches and strife.

The path was straight and clear.
Then distractions along the way caused her to fear.

Somewhere along the route, a detour was taken.
The heart and soul started breakin'.

Slowly things began to change.
All the plans now were rearranged.

High standards once possessed.
The inner being now all bound and stressed.

No more erupting from within.
Sorrow and defeat sure to win.

Accepting anything that came her way.
Yet still fighting not to lose her very identity.

Which Way

No one said it would be easy.
No one said it would all be fun.

No one said no clouds, just sunny.
For behold, here comes a storm.

In life, you have to give and take.
Many decisions you'll have to make.

Some good, some bad,
Others wished you'd never had—

To decide which way to go.
Which way to go?

But someone said it does get better.
"Don't let go, hold tight, hold on."

And He said, "I'm your protector,
And it's all come to make you strong."

In life, you have to give and take.
Many decisions you'll have to make.

Some good, some bad,
Others wished you'd never had—

To decide which way to go.
Which way to go?

What Was It?

Was it an image? Was it pride?
That caused me to smile though my soul had died.

Neglected to balance my account.
When I tried to withdraw it read as insufficient amount.

Belief of horrific case of the blues.
Mission incomplete and hued.

Knowing what I ought to have done
Realizing I should have been up and gone.

Regarding the wrong commands
Suggestions, ideas, and demands.

Was it comfort? Was it security?
That caused loss of vision, yet others could see.

All taking a turn.
After the first go round lesson I assumed learned.

Empty once full.
Still bearing a happy face acting cool.

Discerning fact from fantasy
Reckon mystery.

Perhaps not too late to perceive.

And acquaint assurance once believed.

Outward In

Her face all made up complimented with a smile.
All loved her character as well as her style.

Altogether she had it, so it seemed.
Often spoken of her visions as well as her dreams.

Someone to shadow she was that for me.
In her, I saw the woman I wanted to be.

So strong, so positive, and so caring.
Everything she had you saw her sharing.

Her time, her love, her ear she gave.
No one knew she had a need that she also craved.

Peace in the depths of her soul she did possess.

But something caused her to not be at rest.

Clothes, jewels, and money, enough she had.
The little things in life are what made her glad.

Every morning, she would rise with the sun.
Starting her day by thanking God for all He had done.

But after a full day now drained and tired.
Problems and cares not of her own she retired.

All alone sitting behind those four walls.
An ache from the heart is now recalled.

Fetal position in bed she would lay.
While to her Heavenly Father she would pray.

Tears of sorrow and pain filled her eyes.
It's funny how others considered her a prize.

A void inside she wanted filled.
Wounds from the past also needing to be healed.

Despite all of this it continues to be seen.
She's still loved, respected, and treated like a QUEEN.

The Audition

My name was called. It was my turn.
To show off all over the years learned.

And mastered.
Heart began to beat faster and faster.

Voices running in and out of my head.
Forgot to listen to my heart instead.

I gave it a shot, not 100%.

As if a favor to them lent.

But I was the one cheated,
Since in the audience I am seated.
Realizing

Hurt, scorned and bruised she was
Afraid to open her heart because

She gave her all to that which stole her heart
But one day it decided to depart

All guards at one time where down
Her bright smile, now a frown

Oh the pain she had to endure
Thought that she had was sure

Picking up the pieces trying to go on
Yet realizing all the healing still isn't done.

In the Garden

Planted, buried deep.
Overlooking the soil I was to keep.

Root rot.
Since I ignored, overlooked, forgot.

To develop and plow my own land.
Which initially was the plan.

Instead reaping seeds from another sown.
Adopting ideas and habits not of my own.

Trespassing in their garden.
Robbing, cheating, trying to find a bargain.

Maybe wanting the world to win.
Since destiny set up and said how to have been.

Rejecting the concept of free to be me.

Not living what thought my eyes could see.

Did I choose or was I required?
To obtain not a harvest desired.

To not use tools of my own
Reaping seeds not in my own garden grown.

It Hurts

Let me tell.
It hurts like hell.
But I don't regret it.

I still cry.
Sometimes ask why.
But I don't regret it.

I get mad.
Sometimes sad when I want to be glad.
But I don't regret it.

Disappointed, let down.
Smile momentarily a frown.
But I don't regret it.

A bit disturbed.
Lost for words.
But I don't regret it.

Heart shattered.
Thoughts clattered.
But I don't regret it.

Even right now I feel pain,
Yet so much has been gained.
So I don't regret it.

Yet let me tell.
It hurts like hell.
But I don't regret it.

Someone's Hit

Sorrow, I felt as they bled to death.
Blinked my eyes and an image appeared of self.

Stretched out lying alongside.
With my heart of hearts, I knew why.

I too was dying, being killed.
Or maybe I, myself, silently willed.

To be shot down, cast out.
Delivering a product of doubt.

Since the forged smile upon my face.
Sheltered terror appearing erased.

Making a pathway for assumption.
Nothing standing in need of question.

The hemorrhage constant, it flowed.
Identical to my wounds if exposed.

Fight on

Low my head hung.
As a voice in my ear rung.

And rattled.
Unfolding an unforeseen battle.

Heeding,
Yet bleeding.

For the weight I too carried.
Emotion high and low, it varied.

I too, knew grief, distress, anguish and ache.
Existence from earth appealing to break.

Exchanged blows.
Yet defeat always knows.

Just where to hit next.
Making that which was clear, foggy and complex.

Consider I still stand.
To overcome and complete the plan.

For I'm just being made strong, set up.
To claim and obtain my reward, all my stuff.

Under Construction

Thanks for building me up and not tearing me down.
Don't leave, I will you to stay around.

Thanks for putting a song in my heart and not grief.
Please don't allow your visitation to be brief.

Thanks for encouraging me day to day.
I pray in your heart I will always stay.

Thanks for pushing me without running me over.
And permitting me to lean on your shoulder.

Thanks for being my strength when weak.
And words of life into my spirit you continue to speak.

Gifts inside were stirred and stimulated.
Mind, body and soul all affected, celebrated.

Shuffle the Cards

A stab in the heart is how it felt.
As the next card of life to me was dealt.

Unaware of what was going to be.
But this, no, I couldn't see.

Oh God, my God take this away.
The last draw can I please replay.

I can't take anymore it hurts so bad.
What happened to everything I once had?

Like sand runny through my hands away it went.
Wasted time and energy I guess spent.

Restore the joy I once knew.
That happiness, love and peace too.

Sun please shine through these dark clouds.
Paralyzed by this, I can't allow.

Every time I rise for your rays I look
While seeking to regain that inner strength that was took.

Like a Tree

Rage on storm pour down rain
For its defeats loss and my gain

The mighty winds
May cause my limbs to bend

And maybe even break
But after a good shake

Tall and ready I still stand
Cause and effect of the Creator's plan

Mirrored Image

I pulled my sister to the side
Expressing the need for someone to confide...in

To release some things triggering my mind.
To my surprise I came to find

She not only was an ear
But similar issues she to feared

However, alone she'd been carrying her load
Her mouth didn't say but her emotions told

Just where in life she stood
I couldn't understand how could

She go so long with it all bottled up
As we pulled straws, I figured out what

Had us both hushed thinking it would all disappear
In our eyes it showed really clear

Things glittered but now growing old
Behind closed doors a different story told

Funny how in the other shoes to be we longed

And all this time we were harmonizing, singing the same song

Yet too proud, to puffed up to be real
Fighting and denying what we could really feel

But we could clean up well from head to toe
To everyone else it showed

All was well - all was fine
Had anyone offered just a minute of their time.

A cracked vessel of clay they'd discover
Making them curious and begin to wonder

What's the deal?
It can't be real!

The one that has it going on
Broken down, shaken and torn?

The more you get the happier you are.
The truth be told that is far

From reality
When actually

All that stuff brings about distraction
Causing the soul to get a fraction

A portion of what it's demanding
Not understanding

Those things do bring happiness
But joy is needed in times of stress

Now Hiring

Growing weary and tired.
Wishing my time run out, expire.

Making some sense of this tried.
So complicated won't deny.

Living, moving according to your will.
Yet discouraged once again beginning to feel.

Shed some light in this dark tunnel.
Help me not to complain, bitterly mumble.

Obviously you're in need of a hand.
A voice, a temple a human.

To declare and prove.
You still live and move.

With ALL power.
And blessings still shower.

Grow me up to understand.
All is part of your divine plan.

Grin and Bear

Aiming to be exposed.
Nonetheless, I'm the one nobody knows.

Agreed to the duty conveyed to me.
Inside wanting to leave and them never again see.

Not that instructions I couldn't carry out.
Just finally realizing I could do without.

The demands and request.
Breaking my back to do the best.

Displaying how it should be done.
But it seems it was all in fun.

Since over looked for recommendations
Of rewards, thank you's, presentations.

Who's to blame them or me?
It is I performing regularly.
To accomplish their duties and tasks.

While my agenda remains masked.

Between You and Me

Trust broken; bridges burned.
That's the way lessons learned.

Told to go right, I went left.
Didn't want advice from no one but self.

Advised to look up. I looked down.
So, I went in circles, round and round.

Told to give and I'd receive.
I took and took only concerned with my need.

Told to show love and show myself friendly.
I developed hate and considered you, my enemy.

Now far from the peaceful shore.
Fighting alone in this war.

All those things done to me now bowed down head.
And on bent knees I pled.

Asking for forgiveness and some kind of direction.
For the one once there now displays rejection.

For my guilty charge I've served my time.
Trying to win back what once was mine.

Please open their eyes wide to see.
The new change that's taking over me.

I want to open my heart.
But hard when you're the one who tore it apart.

Now putting the pieces back together.
Hard it is determining whether.

False or true
behind what you now do.

And that you say.
For I let you in back in the day.

Trusting you in my secret spots.
Finding out my spirit would not

Be set free but instead bound.
Wounded and destroyed instead found.

But just like you,
I learned too.

First love me then another.
Oh, you taught me well my brother.

I must be the apple of my own eye.
Be realistic and not live a lie.

I now mean what I say and do as I feel.
To the same God I too kneel.

And direction He has displayed.
Now I'm standing and walking in faith.

Expecting what God had for me.
I love you, but for now I must leave.

Guards Down

Overtaken by the heat.
Accelerated heartbeat.

Hair a mess.
What a good way to relieve some stress.

Torso coated with sweat.
And then our eyes met.

Panting like dogs.
Next time I'll look a little better when I go for a jog.

Halt

So much to do. So little time.
Thousands of thoughts dashing through my mind.

Gotta finish this. Oh, I can't forget that.
Can't think of a single thing to subtract

From this to-do list that has been created.
Along with all the overflow I myself baited.

To absorbed to talk and see how you're doing
Or find out any new things you might be pursuing.

To engrossed to stop and embrace.
No time to spare or put to waste.

Anchored to deep for intimate relations.
Needing to analyze today's notation.

Not right now but possibly tomorrow.
A moment perhaps could be borrowed.

Tomorrow has come but without you.
Oh God, what am I to do?

I took for granted what really mattered most.
Not realizing the high awful cost.

If only I could bend back the hands of time
Priorities would be rearranged and put in line.

Streaming from my eye's tears of sorrow.
Now wishing from yesterday's time to borrow.

Beef Stew

No matter how it's prepared you must have the beef.

I add several seasonings which to myself
I will keep.

Green beans, corn, carrots, sweet peas.
Celery, onion, potatoes I prefer to slice these.

All mixed together simmering on low until hot.
This is my way, now what's in your pot?

Not Known

Had I not failed
I wouldn't be able to tell
And express the true meaning of success.

Had things gone as planned.
I wouldn't know I could withstand
And overcome passing the test.

Out of Sight

No one like me to be found.
Go ahead, take a look around.

No face shaped quite the same.
No one with this matchless frame.

Skin tone of likeness may be familiar.
But the detail throughout, not similar.

It's not the outside that you see
That draws about the curiosity.

The one that's hidden and unseen
Is what stimulates the awe and daydreams.

Strange or odd I'm not going to claim.
But unique, that would be the name

To distinguish what is in the presence before you.
Remarkable, extraordinary, and phenomenal too.

So, to no other could I be compared.
It wouldn't be fair even if you dared.

A peculiar work of art you've just seen.
Created in the likeness of the King of Kings.

Big Girl

I'm a big girl now, all grown up.
Lots of lessons along the way,

Some brought wisdom
Some made me tough.

I'm like a baby bird now ready to fly
Starting low, rising high.

I'm like an infant taking my first step.
Looking and reaching at what's
before me, not to the right or the left.

I'm like a flower in the spring ready to bloom.
Growth and beauty will show through me soon.

I'm like a caterpillar out of the cocoon I'm coming.
Ready to become that mature woman.

I'm like the sun rising on a new day.
Bringing warmth and a smile to all that pass my way.

I'm like an expecting mother delivering a child.
A new me has been birthed, discovered, found.

Yeah, I'm all grown up, big and strong,
Ready this world to take on.

Unwrap It

There's a package, a gift that's wrapped and sealed tight.
It has your name on it, to you and others it will bring delight.

It's not under a tree nor is it any special occasion,
But it sits waiting on your evasion.

The catch is that with your hands you can't obtain it
But I will let you in on the trick.

Start by placing yourself in solitude.
This will help you get in the mood.

Take a deep breath then slowly close your eyes.
Open them back up and look off into the sky.

Now begin to look deep within.
With one glance you'll find you win.

A prize, a gift in which you already own.
See, had you not looked it would have gone unknown.

Remember no two people will stumble upon the same.
So don't let what you find bring about shame.

Unwrap it. Expose it. Master it to the best of your ability.
I dare you to try and solve what's now a mystery.

Tug of War

I pulled and tugged.
In the ground my heels dug.

My grip tightened.
I wasn't going down without fighting.

Since it was mine, all mine.
Ordered it from the Heavenly request line.

Yanked and jerked.
Putting in hard work.

Once out of my hands, snatched,
Dialed that same request line real fast.

Without any holds ups, no interruptions
The voice on the other end asked, "what's the question?"

I sighed.
Then replied,

I thought if I asked, I received.
That's what I was led to believe.

For I was given then robbed.
Now I'm angry and yes, it's me you hear sob.

Hey, hey my child slow down.
I'm glad you stopped, and my number found.

Yes, I gave and now I'm taking it away.
Only because today was the day

To grant that which was greater.
For you have my favor.

Life up your head.
I was listening the other day when you cried and pled.

I'm just coming to your rescue.
Now let it go for there's something greater I have for you.

Feel the Beat

Heel toe, heel toe,
Clack, clack

Heel toe, heel toe
Tap, tap

Clack-a-de-clack
Clack-a-de-clack

Clack, clack
Clack, smack

They glided back and I waltz ahead.
Thought to follow as I was led.

Heel to, heel toe,
Clack, clack

Heel toe, heel toe
Tap, tap

Clack-a-de-clack
Clack-a-de-clack

Clack, clack
Clack, smack

Smack, smack
Tap, smack
Smack-a-de-smack
Clack-a-de-smack

Tap, tap
Tap, tap

Sometimes you must put away the shame.
And step out and do your thang.

Put 'Em Up

Confidence I've found.
Doubt you're about to go down.

That's Friendship

Little moments. Stolen moments we shared them both.
Despite which of the two, LOVE was the host.

Conversation began on the surface.
Within days discovering this relationship had purpose.

Oh, how we would laugh.
And I remember at times we'd have

Tears in our eyes.
Sharing not our opinions but what was wise.

Since several issues shared.
Confessing them we dared.

For a season things got tough.
Not knowing, we held the other up.

With encouraging words and acts of kindness
We reassured the other that even the wildest

Of dreams can and do come true.
Giving up we just couldn't do.

Yet another crossroad you stand.
Open my heart and stretched my hand.

You will find
For you are a special friend of mine.

Strength in Weakness

At first glimpse sorrow grasped.
Watching as his hands clasped.

That which substituted his limbs.
The second look I saw a grin.

Then a smile, wow!
How

Is it that my head hung so low,
Free to do and free to go

At my discretion.
Yet worrying, doubting full of frustration.
Whining since life didn't seem fair.
Looked at him again trying not to stare.

Then asked of self, suppose
This man gave up and chose

To live a life of pity?
Sitting on his gifts instead of giving?

Evidently he had found his divine place.
Since a smile was even brought to my face.

Designed it was for our paths to cross.
Not knowing, he handed me back that which I had tossed.

A Met Need

Just when I wanted to give in.
God sent my way a friend.

One who listened when I talked.
Expressing what was and wasn't my fault.

One who gave wise advice.
Convincing me not to be naughty but nice.

A pat on the back they would give.
Causing me to realize the true meaning of this life I live.

But when they weren't around
I knew their knees where on the ground,

Hands together and a bowed down head,
Petitioning the Lord not for self but for me instead.

As if the Seasons

The spring showers
Assist flourishing of the flowers.

The summer sun
Trigger all to seek and find fun.

The fall breeze
Cause trees to lose their leaves.

The winter snow
Transform swift paces to slow.

There are gifts and talents buried inside
That we ignore and subside.

Just as the seasons change so must I.
Some by choice, others not clear why.

However, it's a good thing.
Allowing time to bring

Fresh ideas and endeavors.
And make way to favors

Above and beyond that which I can envision.
Permitting me to fulfill my mission.

And recognize what really matters to me.
Compelling me to be nothing but happy!

Simple Things

It's the simple things that caused me to think.
You know how you would look at me and your left eye would blink.

Walking through the park holding hands.
And how to our own music we would dance.

Mmm, I love how you would graze my face.

Then smother me in that constricted embrace.

Staring at one another, making goo goo eyes.
And all the worries and cares of this world that bothered us dies

Away...just for a season.
Since at that moment one another we were pleasing.

Funny how from within I would just melt
And your touch not even yet felt.

At that moment that is, because when you did,
Unconsciously I would close my eyelids.

Bite my bottom lip then slowly slide out my tongue.
Caressing you softly hoping you'd come

Closer, that is, not wanting no distance between us
Because the feeling was, mmm just…

out of this world unlike no other.
My all you had my brother.

You had me screaming but no one else could hear
Even though it sounded off loud and clear.

We knew that from the inner vessel it came
And this place, no man or nothing could never, ever tame.

Dance I Said

And dance and snap your fingers too.
Know nothing matters as long as you're happy with who

You are and who you're becoming,
Along with the wisdom you share yet still learning.

Do your thang,
And don't be shame.

For it makes the soul glad
And happy the face that once was sad.

Even if into your world one tries to peak,
With your head up keep moving to the beat.

For they're just curious of what it is
That has you carrying on like you do and with such confidence.

If they'd just tune in to their concealed tempo
They could join you too on the flo'.

Until the last jam is played,

Keep carrying on, letting nothing stop you from doing it your way.

Free-Dome

You may not like it
But I love it.

If you were honest
You'd find that you covet,

And envy,
Desiring one day to be like me.

Not my temple, in my dome.
Although loose ends need to be sewn

Together and others put in place.
The attitude, the mentality of finishing the race

Has you stunned, has you astounded.
Since just like an Olympic swimmer, it's been noted.

Once into the deep waters I dove,
Poise continued to hold.

With each stroke more determination delivered.
Only the finish line considered.

Scripture says it's not the strong or swift who wins
But the one who endures until the end.

Go Get It

I sense an appetite for something greater.
You should really satisfy that crave now, why wait until later?

Arms opened, unlocked, extended but right now, you just stand.
Go ahead, be aggressive, persistent
At that which you demand.

Desire, want and need all subsist and are in line.
To absorb that which will quench
fulfill and make all fine.

You're looking out into the deep waters while you stand at the shore.
I can see it in your eyes that you really want more.

Try closing your eyes and then take a deep breath.
Slowly open them but don't look to your right or your left.

Only what's in front of you should be in sight.
Yet, fear, nervousness, wonder may try to trip you up, it just might.

But due to your known character, determination, energy and drive.
I know that you'll be fine once you take that dive.

Go on

No, it wasn't easy.
But man, it is pleasing,

And encouraging to witness you've arrived.
To a point that many have and still strive.

Much relief you must feel.
Yesterday's dream today is real.

At times I know it was tough.
On edge wanting to give up.

But thanks to the Heavenly Father
For not letting you be bothered.

Nor sifted like wheat
By that enemy known as defeat.

Instead, you held up your head
Keeping a vision instead.

Right in front of you all the way.
Now look at your today.

More mountains to climb are in store.
But that's fine, it'll allow you to shine once more.

Great Expectation

I can't see it nor figure out how it will come to pass.
But if I can just hold out a little longer, just last

A little more, that one door
I'm so eagerly waiting to open will reveal all and more.

I know it's coming. It's as if I can feel it in my bones.
Despite my standing here in solitude, alone.

For many started off by my side

But hindered by a mind not opening wide.

And doubt arresting
Even though from the mouth confessing

They too had what it took.
Yet knocked by a hard breeze that came and shook

Things up a bit
Causing some to whine and have a fit.

But for me, I'm standing on a strong foundation.
For I've got great expectations.

She in Me

Entering the room demanding attention.
Dressed to kill I should mention.

Gracefully moving through the crowd.
Poised, sweet and pleasant not out of control or wild.

Objective distributed with confidence and surety.
Inside and out just sho' nuff pretty.

Virtuous this woman, one of honor and respect.
Fruits of the spirit she did reflect.

Warmth given to that which was cold.
Value greater than that of silver or gold.

No dollar amount could be attached.
A written check couldn't even be cashed.

For her wealth is far too great.
This rare jewel, hard to find a duplicate.

There are some in which many come close.
Which is how I'm watching, hoping, suppose,

The time the spotlight shines on me
In her footsteps I can follow ever so closely.

Hidden Treasure

You may or may not like what you see.
But hold up, there's more to me.

I'm not your average or ordinary female.
Ya see, there's a multitude of hidden details.

Now, I enjoy and find pleasure being on my back.

Yet don't be surprised, knowledge I don't lack.
Beautiful I'm told to the organ of sight.
However, what you can't see gives me such hype.

I can sit tight and look cute sitting in your ride.
Do know that any topic that comes up I can vibe.

I can support your visions and dreams.
I too, am working on pulling a few strings.

It's not that I'm arrogant or puffed up.
Not cocky, boastful or physically tough.

The secret, I was introduced to the one inside.
Didn't realize the depth of my soul and all that abides.

Here the real and true me dwells.

I possess the keys to release it from its cell.

For so long never knew of such a thing.
But now the door is unlocked unspeakable joy sings.

So busy primping and preparing the exterior being.
Ignorant of the fact the one out of sight needed feeding.

Striving to be life all the rest.
Making sure I passed the physical test.

I found out that if I first love me,
Everyone else would notice my inner beauty.

A hidden treasure could be the name.
The killer part is that we all have the same.

If you haven't already acquainted yourself,
Hurry quickly while there's a little time left.

I Imagined

I imagined tears of sorrow no more
I imagined being explored

I imagined healed hurt
I imagined ideas birthed

I imagined a mended heart
I imagined a new start

I imagined being encouraged
I imagined finding that I searched

I imagined consistency
I imagined a heard plea

I imagined a smile brought upon my face
I imagined winning the race

I imagined being looked into my eyes
I imagined breaking ties

I imagined the truth being told
I imagined love unconditional

I imagined releasing that I held in
I imagined totally surrendering

I imagined off guard being caught
I imagined winning that which I fought

I imagined loosening total control
I imagined return of that which was stole

I imagined a hand being lent
I imagined giving 100 percent

I imagined dreams becoming realities
I imagined just being me

Help

Deliver to and deduct from my life as you see fit.
As I progress day to day venturing to find my niche.

Grant wisdom to crown my head.
Causing others to resurrect from the dead.

Develop my voice, influential and clear.
So, I can dispense the words my brothers and sisters need to hear.

Purge my heart, make it oh so pure.
This way folks will discern I'm genuine, they'll be sure.

Empower to not look at others through natural eyes.
This will help to exclusively see that prize

That he or she had concealed inside.
One's, they didn't even identify or recognize.

Entitle ways to probe and challenge their minds.
And that chaotic and tangled life unwind.

Bestow patience and stick-to-it-ness.
While unto me they pour out sorting through the mess.

A measure of mercy and grace I need.
Hungry souls I desire to feed.

Available and ready I am to win some souls.
Bringing back even those that where stole.

You've been better to me than I've been to myself.
Now Lord, help me be a blessing and stand in the gap for someone else.

Shoe Shine

I gazed in awe.
As from his hip he reached to draw

This stain filled rag.
"Like new, like new" he ranted and bragged.

With a frowned face
And curiosity embraced,

I paused
Wondering the cause

Of the excitement and all the fuss.
And in line folk rushed.

There in hand was positioned these shoes.
Long walks, they'd endured a few.

The sole was worn and terribly damaged.

Should've been thrown in Tuesday night's garbage.

The toe badly scratched and scuffed.
And if that wasn't enough

The heels were condensed on the left side.
My slanted eyes stretched wide

As he began to remove and replace.
With expectancy I chased

His craftiness, his skill.
My attention still

Focused.
One might say nosey, cause

I was zoned
And couldn't leave this situation alone.

Then the rag began to snap and pop.
And left then right his shoulders rocked.

The tip toe began to reflect a ray of the sun.
And he bellowed out, "Take a look I'm done!"

Just like that restoration had occurred.
And I had assumed and preferred

To make them history
But looks like they have a few more blocks to see.

Delight Disorder

I need to act my age
Was the phrase

Mentioned
As a vision

Of the days to come where created.
Really planned and organized it was laid

And spelled out.
Yet once again proceeded out of the mouth.

I'm too old to carry on this way.
But a different message actions displayed.

But who and what's to say
When hearts desire should be betrayed?

Left unnoticed as if not there.
Denying self which isn't fair.

Since it won't disappear.
It's like a battle that creates this crazy fear.

A fear that develops into a disease.
You know the one to please

Everyone else.
The very ones that aren't happy themselves.

So then who's living for who?
Who's to say what one can and cannot do

At any stage of life.

Struggling to grab a piece of the pie and take a bite.

The pie that represents possibilities and opportunities.
Goals, visions and dreams.

Sad that many will never know
All that life had to show

And reveal.
Just because they began to feel

That time had run out
Leaving them to wonder and doubt.

If yesterday's pillow talk
Today's path walked.

And just to taste the pie
But left long faced not giving it a try.

Mother's Touch

Seems so touchy feely.
Somewhat greedy along with needy.

Wanting much attention.
And not to mention.

In attendance a longing
For someone, something to make him

feel some kind of belonging.
So much so, you could say selfish since

always trying to fill his cup.
But in other instances portraying this
facade of tough man.

You had to know him to understand
Thank brick wall and harsh tone
Where lyrics, the bridge to his midnight
song.

As if a cry without the physical tears.
Or the shiver, that shake caused by that
he feared.

He would labor from sun up to sun
down throughout the week.
Discreetly tasting substitute nectar of
that he seeked.

A loner and somewhat secretive.
If asked for his last he'd freely give.

All these years there was an idea of love.
A need for love.
A release of love.

A display of love.
An existence of love

But what had hi bound in such a clutch?
It was the absence of that mother's touch.

A mother's voice. a mother's ear.
A mother's warm hug to hold him near.

Others have played the role and played it well,
But not well enough to the soul sell.

For there is a difference.
And it plays a big part in one's existence.

Those years have passed and cannot be bought back.

So now he walks this earth trying to get on track.

Wanting to give but how much?
Wanting to take but when's enough?

Wanting to open up but with who?
Just wanting love that's sure and true.

My Brother, My Lover, My King

I see you, I see you trying to break from that cell.
Been some time since the outside you've been able to dwell.

But keep tryin', keep diggin', you're almost there.
Wait, what happened you're back where you started, you got nowhere.

C'mon, c'mon, stop blaming it all on Dan.
Put up the violins, take responsibility, take charge, I know you can

Break from those claims, come out of the darkness, end the struggle,
I know, I know all the pieces haven't been found to complete the puzzle.

Yeah, they said there would be good days as well as the bad.
But have you noticed so much energy is wasted being angry and mad.

Evidently you haven't figured out the POWER in which you possess.
If you really knew there's no way you would settle for less.

Aww, there you go, I think you've found the key.
I think you've figured it out, I'm looking at you and I can see

A change in action, a change in thinking, a change indeed.
To use your mind not sharp words and quick blows was the need.

Now as you continue to build on this new foundation you've laid,
A shoulder, an ear, a voice, I'm there to your aid.

To be free lies in you but as your Queen I play a big part as well.
I can give you heaven on earth or I can make it seem like hell.

Didn't always know I helped and contributed in holding you down, keeping you bound.
A duplicate of the key to that cell was in my possession thanks to God I now have found.

See, I've tapped into that power I mentioned to you at the beginning.
I too, was angry, mad, disgusted, a captive imprisoned.

Now I love myself for who I am and who I'm becoming.
Self doubt, low self-esteem, depression, see all that I've overcome.

So I stretch out my hand and words of life only will I speak.
For you've been through too many heartaches and born having to defeat.

No more tearing you down starting right now I'm going to build you up.
You're going to be something, something GOOD and BIG, folks just won't get enough.

You're on your way. I'm on my way and we determine how high.
There's no stopping us now for the limit is beyond the sky!

Nicci Roach is an award-winning professional in learning and development, strategy, and leadership. She is an accomplished author, educator, and entrepreneur, dedicated to equipping leaders to create more inclusive and diverse spaces.

Nicci is the principal of Covenant exCHANGE, LLC, founder of CLOUT, and host and producer of Conversations in the Nic of Time, a talk-radio show. Holding advanced degrees in public relations, human resources, and media communications, as well as certifications in leadership and diversity, Nicci is currently completing her doctorate in Higher Education Leadership, furthering her mission to inspire and empower through interactive lectures, consulting, and media.

NicciRoach.com

www.ingramcontent.com/pod-product-compliance
Lightning Source LLC
LaVergne TN
LVHW021045250325
806728LV00050B/263